T0129898

THE BREADTH
OF A TREE

THE BREADTH OF A TREE

Poems, Letters, and Dreams

i. peaches gillette

iUniverse®

THE BREADTH OF A TREE
POEMS, LETTERS, AND DREAMS

Author Credits: Tanja Schubert, cover redesign
James LaVeck, photo
Lauren Basciani, peach-blossom drawings

iUniverse books may be ordered through booksellers or by contacting:

iUniverse
1663 Liberty Drive
Bloomington, IN 47403
www.iuniverse.com
1-800-Authors (1-800-288-4677)

ISBN: 978-1-5320-2116-9 (sc)
ISBN: 978-1-5320-2115-2 (e)

Library of Congress Control Number: 2017906796

Print information available on the last page.

iUniverse rev. date: 10/08/2018

DEDICATION

He saw my passion for writing and did everything
in our physical and emotional world to create
the room for me to live this passion.

This book of poems, letters, and dreams is
preciously dedicated to my husband,
Peter John Thomas,
who is the coauthor of our love for each
other that we began writing
more than thirty-six years ago.

May our story continue to be written.

FOREWORD BY MARYAM LOWEN

Peaches and I met in a church basement in Brooklyn many years ago; it was 1978. We were there to make poems.

I was a teacher, a dancer, and a poet. I had a new baby, and I did not have a job. I had received a $300 writing grant from Poets & Writers to teach a workshop at Project Reach Youth (PRY), a youth organization housed in the Park Slope United Methodist Church. That $300 was my entire earnings for the year. It was the holiest money I ever earned. To earn money that could buy food and subway tokens in exchange for making poems was shocking. Incredible. The way I wanted life to be.

About ten years later, I was in the living room of another poet friend's house in San Francisco, gazing in awe and appreciation at the book-lined walls, marveling at her bookshelves filled with her very own published works. *Poetry bought this house!* I thought. This same friend is now a well-known American novelist, short-story writer, poet, and activist who has won a Pulitzer Prize for her work.

I saw in the real world that a real person who was my friend had placed her dreams and feelings into shapes that could be transmitted to others. She had built a world of bricks and paint and windows from those dreams. Poems . . . another word for dreams.

Now, about thirty-six years later, Peaches's dreams and poems have grown and grown. They have attached themselves to paper or electronic screens. The poem about sounds that we wrote the first day we met has burgeoned. She listened: She heard the pipes crackling; the children's pencils and pens tapping and scratching; vehicles rolling by at street level, above our quiet haven.

Her words and sounds have swelled. This time she listened to the world and heard it fully. Captivated by its wonders. Bursting to share them with any who care to venture in.

To hear and see and feel what Peaches does. Welcome.

June 30, 2016
a Thursday

SILENCE

(Fifteen-minute writing assignment, 1978)

The distant whispers of people talking, the creaking in this old chair, the humming of something mechanical, something electric.

I hear the steps of someone I cannot see, and the tinkling of Maryam's bracelets, the turning of pages. The muffled sound that comes from my pen or pencil when I am writing, the many suppressed thoughts in my head and the pieces of songs and old, almost forgotten memories all trying to escape. My toes cracking inside my boots; there is always something to be heard. Never is it really silent.

A cough echoing through this cold, musty basement, my fingers scratching my forehead.

Silence is made up of the sounds that lie within the silence.

The pipes banging as something passes through them, more whispers. The sounds of all the silence being stored in my head. The dragging of a purse across a table, many more songs: "And when you know that you've got a real friend somewhere, suddenly all the others are so much easier to bear." I sing out softly.

The sound of a broom sweeping the concrete floor. The wooden part of the broom tapping against chair legs. I faintly hear the sound of traffic from above. I wonder if it could ever be completely silent. I doubt it.

The sound of my own breathing, the sound of my spit being swallowed.

Some of the best noises are the sound of tearing paper, the whispers of others, meters clicking, heartbeats, car horns, forearms sliding back and forth across notebooks, the sound of my fillings settling every time I clench my teeth, the sound of doorbells, the sound of a familiar voice, the air as it forces its way in and out of my nostrils, the slamming of a heavy door, my fist slowly sliding down my face across my hair.

By Peaches Gillette

ACKNOWLEDGMENTS

It is through loving others that I find spiritual freedom,
and it is through the beauty of this special kind of freedom
that I am compelled to write myself down
and to share that writing with others.

I am happy I have the opportunity to name names and
to say a word or two about the people in my life who have
inspired me in the most complete sense of the word;
through the power of their friendship,
they breathed life into me,
and I, in turn, breathed life into this book.

I thank each of you for keeping my soul astir
with hope and my world filled with love.

To my friends Jenny Stein and James LaVeck for always holding high the light of humanity, for hearing the cries of the world with their hearts and responding to those cries through their impassioned documentaries. I extend a special thank-you to James for guiding me through some of the technical content of this book and for keeping me true to myself as a writer by simply saying, "That sounds more like the Peaches I know." To Elizabeth Mae Hudson (my mother) for teaching me to love well and to believe that each of us can create miracles for one another; and to my son, Jamel Gillette, his lovely wife Victoria, and their children,

Alexis, Gianna, and Brianna, for providing me a place to rest that love. To my good friend and jazz guitarist David Ullmann, whose gentle soul has always made me think that there was hope in this world. To my dear friend Anida Sangkala, who sparks faith in everyone by never, ever giving up. To my love Zumoi Jones, who was the inspiration behind the poem She/Beautiful Dancer, and to all my other children friends who keep me tenderly close to the most meaningful parts of my own childhood and who power the world with their love and laughter. To Professor Leslie Satan, who once said to me, "Just write. You are a writer."

To Tanja Schubert, who invited me to her childhood home in Germany to share her story with me; her beautiful friendship was the beginning of a new and profoundly meaningful chapter in my life. I also thank Tanja for taking my vision of the book cover and actualizing it. To my sweet Donna Slack-Barketey (and her perfect family), who is the proverbial unsung artist, a great laugher, and the one who provides me with the opportunity to be "cool by association." To Lauren Basciani, my niece through marriage, for coming through in a pinch with the beautiful peach-blossom drawings. To the women at Bedford Correctional Facility, who stepped into my heart and expanded my understanding of compassion and forgiveness. To Malachi Gillette, my nephew, just because I have always loved him. To Robyn Bem, author, editor, and friend, whose professional input helped move this book into publication. And to my dear Peter, who only interrupted my writing frenzy to bring me tea and nibbles.

To Daulton, who I met only in a dream but who became a very real and meaningful part of my life; you will always stay lovingly in my heart. Rest peacefully, dear friend. To John Lyon Paul and his wife Katherine Kiblinger, who swaddled me with their love and friendship during a very dark time in my life.

Finally, I thank my beloved friend and poet Maryam Lowen. In both spirit and body, she was with me during the deep and emotional process of transforming a dream into reality. Like an angel in flight, she flew down from Michigan over the summer of 2016, and for four weeks she stayed at my home in Brooklyn, working tirelessly day and night—my poet-guide who walked beside me every step of the way along my path toward becoming a published poet. Our time together was intense, exhausting, exhilarating, and brilliant—our creative energy on fire—our friendship tempered like steel. And although the summer has passed, our walk together as poets and as friends continues; it is the same walk that we began together in the church basement in Brooklyn in 1978.

INTRODUCTION

The Breadth of a Tree

For as far back as I can remember, trees have had an enduring effect on me; something has always drawn me to them. Trees not only represented my mother's childhood, but they have come to represent my own, creating a beautiful and symbolic parallel of our lives—one that has a powerful emotional charge for me and is what created my connection to this special life form.

I remember my mother, Elizabeth Mae Hudson, telling us stories about her life growing up in the country—a life I grew to love and yearned to have because of her. Although she was born in Baltimore, Maryland, a large part of her childhood and most of her early adulthood were spent in the backlands of South Carolina.

My mother's life was not easy, but as it is for most people, no matter how difficult life might be, there are moments in their childhood that feel enchanted. She enjoyed playing outside in open fields, searching for ghost trains that were said to be heard passing through the woods, and was quite skilled at climbing trees. Her stories connected me to the wonders of her childhood, who she was as a person, and where she had come from.

My mother was very plain in looks and was beautifully natural. Everything about her spoke to me of a simplicity that was unique then (when I was a child) and still is. Her simplicity kept me connected to nature, to things that were left untampered and untouched. She was a calm woman, whose firmest opinions were expressed respectfully and sympathetically. But no amount of simplicity can stop the challenges that one must face in this world.

My mother grew up in abject poverty, a Black woman born in America in 1911. She labored on farmlands in the South, did domestic work, and could barely survive from day to day. She had seen the ugliest side of inequality and had experienced the often-brutal systems of racism that were (are) designed for the sole purpose of dominating and crushing the spirit. She saw the lives of her own parents and many others around her destroyed by the gravity of severe privation and racial oppression. But somehow, throughout all the adversity and hardship, throughout the emotional and physical toil and the pain, she remained true to who she was—a woman who held onto the belief that you steadfastly fight the good fight of faith, you let your actions be guided by truth and justice, and you treat others the way you would want to be treated, no matter what. She was a woman who stood strong; who never gave up; who lived with her eyes facing heaven and her arms reaching lovingly out to the world. That was the nature of my mother, and as a child, I saw so many of her qualities reflected within nature itself, within the nature of trees—within their simplicity and their strength.

One of my other intimate relationships with trees formed because they were a prominent part of my childhood landscape. Although I grew up in New York City—Park Slope, Brooklyn, to be specific—I lived only two short blocks from Prospect Park, a place that seemed like an endless kingdom of hills and trees. Most all children in our neighborhood spent at least 75 percent of their time in the park and the other 25 percent playing street games on our block. Park Slope was a neighborhood made up of rows of homes with front yards of potted shrubs and flowers that sat on sidewalks lined with trees.

The Title

Poems and titles of poems often appear as a single thought or a random phrase that lies within the psyche for an unpredictable amount of time, seemingly gestating, waiting to be fully born. So many of the poems in this book have come into the world this way, and it was no different for the title. Recently, someone asked me why I chose this particular title for my book. They were, understandably, unable to grasp my relationship with trees—considering that I spent my entire life in a big city—nor could they grasp the relationship between the content of this book and the title itself.

For me, the question I was asked should not have revolved around trying to find out why I would choose a title for my book that is focused on a tree but what it is about a tree that made it central to the title.

Thank You for Asking

After a long day of work and errands, I often sit at my desk at home, lean back in my chair, and use the time to think, write, and reflect on my experiences over the course of my life. Right outside the window, across the street but in plain sight, stands a glorious tree, tall and with a broad crown. It is often the focus of my daydreaming and my unending nostalgia. One day I found myself contemplating its beauty and detailing its specialness. I thought about the number of branches it takes for a tree to produce such a large crown and, metaphorically speaking, how "the many" can arise from a few or even from one. I found this thought to be a deep point of identity for me as a person with many selves arising from one self. I then began contemplating the structure of the self and became increasingly curious about the general structure of a tree and the number of branches a tree can produce.

I learned through a bit of research that there are two types of tree growth that produce the greatest crowns. The first is a tree whose breadth (of both trunk and crown) is the result of its species and its age. The second, classified as multi-trunk, is a tree that has several trunks.

A multi-trunk tree forms when the original stems or shoots of the tree are somehow damaged; they may have been browsed upon by animals (including insects), broken in storms, or abused by humans. They often continue to grow as the result of smaller shoots or individual trunks that develop to compensate for what was lost. The new growth is part of a one-root mass that has separate trunks with one base, or the individual trunks have become fused together. This is a sacred sight for me. Trees are breathtaking; their crowns can be magnificent in the truest sense of the word, and their girth enormous. I feel in awe— nature is so amazing—an attestation of how life will not be easily diminished.

I ponder this occurrence in nature not only from a botanical and biological point of view but from a spiritual one as well. I see a profound similarity between the process that takes place in the natural world of trees and my own evolution. My development into a person with many selves emerged out of the innate aptitude to survive no matter what damage, large or small, may have been done. The phrase "the breadth of a tree" came into my thoughts. The breadth of a tree is a perfect example of the growth that takes place over time even against countless odds.

A Story Continued

The flow of traffic on the block where I live faces the east, one block away from Prospect Park. As I drive along looking for parking, the view before me is the park itself and the breathtaking arch of trees that overhang the street. For me, these trees readily become a serene point of convergence for my ideating, ruminating, and meditating; no matter how many layers of thought are shifting about in my mind, one of them is always in recognition of how visibly captivating the trees are and how they move and sound when the wind is just right.

One evening, as I drove along my block, the phrase "the breadth of a tree" quietly reappeared in my thoughts. I found it replaying in endless loops for weeks thereafter. It was a phrase that continued to have emotional value and that I began to feel needed a place to live, a context. It was me again but in a different way. It was a simple phrase, but like me, it seemed to be eternally searching for a place to live in this not-so-simple world, and so I made the decision that *The Breadth of a Tree* would be a perfect title for this book.

I love trees. Even without the intimate association they have for me in relation to my mother and to my childhood, I find myself in awe of both their timelessness here on earth and their dual quality of being gentle yet strong. I love the way the shade of a tree is cool and merciful, unlike any other type of shade. I love the way the leaves sound as they are blown by the wind or dropped upon by the rain. I love the way trees look silhouetted by a darkened sky or backlighted by the moon. I love the way they are a life that gives life and home to others—like mothers do.

This book, this collection of my writings, is my many selves put down on paper. Each piece represents the spiritual, internal, multiple parts of who I am—my thoughts, my feelings, my life, and the experiences I have had that continue to expand the breadth of my existence. As I present myself to you, the reader, through the various poems, letters, dreams, dream poems, and reflections, understand that I am not simply sharing my writing with you; I am inviting you into my heart. Welcome to *The Breadth of a Tree.*

CONTENTS

Poems

Sonnets

Dream Poems

Letters

Dreams

POEMS

*I would define, in brief, the poetry of words
as the rhythmical creation of beauty.*

—Edgar Allan Poe

I recall being very quiet and self-conscious for as far back as I can remember; this was my personality until I was in my late twenties. I shied away from even the shortest conversations, always feeling that I did not know what to say or how to say it. I was terrified about the possibility of my thoughts and feelings being misunderstood, rejected, or laughed about. I convinced myself that no one would want to hear what I had to say, and so to a large extent, I withdrew from the world around me to protect myself emotionally. Doing this left me feeling as if I only partially existed, but I eventually discovered that reading became a way to feel that I existed more fully.

I read most everything I could. I was excited when I received reading assignments from school or when I salvaged books that people in the neighborhood discarded; I was introduced to Bradbury and Sterling in this way. I read all the poetry of Edgar Allan Poe and Walt Whitman. I fell in love with the idea of putting feelings down on paper. To me, it was far less risky than speaking. From reading, I fell in love with writing. I wanted to capture the ability to put emotions into words with the freedom that writing seemed to allow. Poetry ended up being the style of writing that was most gratifying to me. The art of fitting so much beauty and feeling within the structure of a poem fascinated me, and so poetry became an important way that I could give myself a voice.

Writing gave me the room to speak and to be soundless at the same time, to privately express myself without worrying about my emotional awkwardness or risking being misunderstood; it provided a place of retreat during the times when I needed to do so. Writing was a perfect way to not think or worry about knowing what to say.

The silence of writing in general and of writing poetry feels right to me. The process requires sitting with my thoughts and doing a spiritual examination of all that I feel, see, and believe. No matter how much emotion rises to the surface, writing is settling; it is quieting—a meditative and reflective activity that gives me the chance to express my love, my gratitude, my fears, and my connection to nature and to the world around me.

The poems, letters, and dreams in this book are a humble way to share myself with you.

SEVENTH STREET

We were as wild as grass and as free as the wind,
and life felt big and endless.

Each summer brought a special kind of warmth
that swept us up into its arms and rescued us
from wooden desks
and cardboard teachers.

The world of Seventh Street was full of possibilities,
full of the sound and smell
of 5:00 a.m. garbage trucks
machine-humming us into a new day.

Was full of blueprints of rockets sketched
by the imagination of a child
and stickball bats and rooftop home runs.

Was full of curious eyes
watching city workers replace squares of broken sidewalk
and eager hands waiting to press prints
onto the freshly poured pavement.

Was full of sidewalk games and jump-rope songs
and bottle caps packed with tar

ready to be thumb-clicked across chalk-drawn skelsy boards
that decorated the asphalt.

Life was big,
and we filled our days
with the business of childhood.

We played.

We stood on piles of sunlight and laughter and
listened to our souls echo off the walls of our
childhood dreams of never-ending summers.

We played.

Life was the hard, smothering concrete
and we the wild grass growing from between the cracks—
stretching toward the sun.
And in our endless playing,
and in our ceaseless dreaming,
we found togetherness,
and we found something even more.

We found sacred intervals
where the angry hands of alcoholic fathers could not reach us.

We found hallowed places
where the tear-stained faces of our
struggling mothers did not pain us.

We found solemn realms
where poverty had no power and the harsher parts of living

were not able to rip into our hearts
or weaken our spirits.

We found guarded emotional territories in
which we were simply allowed to be—
an opening in time where time itself
stood perfectly still
just for us.

We found hope in the freedom to play,
and so we played,
and we dreamed,
and we hoped.

And that hope was what carried us through each day
and through each year, for many years
until the world of Seventh Street
eventually faded away with our youth—
slowly dissolved,
vanished,
weeping,
as if it were just a dream.

ANOTHER YEAR

Each day,
each year that passes
grants us another opportunity to come of age,
to renew our thoughts,
to center ourselves as we continue our journey.

Our bodies, our minds, and life itself
shift and change,
and so must our relationship with the world around us.

Mourning over what we feel we have lost
as we move through time
and as time moves through us
can be a painful process,
a temporal reminder that we must begin
to let go.

But understand
that in letting go
we are able to hold on
to the chance to gain perspective,
to expand our understanding of those closest to us
and of ourselves.

We attach tenderly to our own histories
and perhaps become more compassionate toward others
as they move through their own time.

We might be reminded
that if our lives are at all measured
by the love we have,
even for the things we've lost,
then our lives
in essence
are truly timeless.

This is what we are left with;
time *will* pass.
And so let us use the days we have before us
to remember,
to celebrate,
and to appreciate
all that we once had,

And as we do so,
let us not allow the time we spend reflecting on yesterday
make us forget all that we still have today.

A SUMMARY OF SORROWS

A Journal of My Thoughts
South Carolina, July 17, 2016

A death within a dream.
A simple prophesy.

A bridge I had to cross.
A journey toward an end.

A dear friend that I missed.
A yearning to go home.

A lynching in a book.
A place where time stood still.

A brother that I loved.
A life I could not save.

A haunting breeze that blew.
A whisper from the past.

A history undone.
A people left behind.

A calling from the ocean.
A world from whence I came.

A rising sound within me.
A voice that no one heard.

A road that I must travel.
A direction never found.

A tree broad and inviting.
A bird that could not see.

A daughter skilled in hatred.
A father turned away.

A mountain in the distance.
A lonely silhouette.

A time I can't go back to.
A child I kissed good-bye.

A day that never ended.
An inscription left in blood.

A young life drenched in sorrow.
A world too sad to bear.

A final breath repeated.
A ghost I had become.

A friendship filled with malice.
A painful certainty.

An apology to the universe.
A well that had gone dry.

A black hole deep inside me.
A need to be set free.

A soul I came to cherish.
A stranger in a cage.

A funeral continued.
A family paralyzed.

A thundering sky above me.
A child held in my arms.

An electrifying rainfall.
A chill throughout the night.

A flash across the darkness.
A shattering of faith.

A suicide at sunrise.
A sacrificial lamb.

A lifetime to unravel.
An ending understood.

A cry within the belly.
A place I'll always know.

A debt that can't be settled.
A grave of broken bones.

A fire unattended.
A kinship turned to ash.

A poem I had written.
A song that broke my heart.

A world that was ill-suited.
A purpose never known.

A photo I remembered.
A portrait of a loss.

A prayer that was discarded.
A wound that never healed.

A body old and weary.
A point of no return.

A woman slowly dying.
A man with nothing left.

A spirit bound to suffer.
A disinvested God.

A reminder of our failings.
A planet lost in space.

A holocaust in motion.
A bell that tolls for thee.

A ripple in the cosmos.
An echo in my soul.

A body I'll surrender.
A truth I apprehend.

An existence full of anguish.
A howl before the dawn.

A summary of sorrows.
A journal of my thoughts.

A CONVERSATION WITH GIANNA

Myrtle Beach, South Carolina
July 18, 2016—7:35 p.m.

I realize
that she talks a lot about death.
I believe she's trying to figure it out,
comprehend what it really means,
sort out how to feel about it,
emotionally qualify
and quantify its overall effects.

I haven't really figured it out either.
Maybe it's no more complicated
than what a four-year-old understands
or doesn't understand.

On the beach in South Carolina,
she heard someone talking about sharks;
she heard her older sister talking about sharks;
she heard a man talking about having
taken a picture of a shark,
a large shark that he had spotted
in the distance.

Over dinner,
she told me about the man who saw a shark.
In her version of the story,
a princess was found dead on the beach that day,
having bled to death from a shark bite.

According to her,
this tragedy took place
very close to where she was
playing in the sand
and jumping over waves.
I told her,
my voice soaked in sorrow,
that this was the saddest story I'd ever heard
and that we would make sure
she was safe in the water
and in the world.

She looked at me, her expression somber,
a sadness on her face.
She simply stared into my eyes
and then looked away.

She told me about her mother having a cousin who "got dead."
She told me that the cousin went to heaven.
I asked her
if heaven was a good place.
She told me no
because everyone there had died.

EXQUISITE

I saw Jenny after she had navigated her
way across the enormous road,
overwhelmed by the mercilessness of the traffic.
Her expression was that of distress and fright.
I should have been with her; some things
should not be done alone.

She sat in the front seat of the car.
Her voice was shaky, and the movement of her
emotions came out in word-sounds
that let James and me know how disquieting and
worrying the experience was for her.
I listened from the seat behind her and
reached forward to touch her shoulder,
to stroke her shoulder,
to pass a sense of peace back into her heart.

How fragile and delicate she seemed—

not in a way that exposes weakness,
but in a way that exposes the character of a person
who accesses this special part of
herself,
the part of herself that is characteristically exquisite,

that allows her to be intimate with her
own sense of vulnerability,
that allows her to trust that others will care
and will sensitively respond.

I found myself in awe of her,
moved by her gentle, sensitive soul.
I envied her freedom to feel unsafe and frightened
and to believe that she could find comfort.

It was a feeling that I never had the privilege of having.

FORGIVENESS

Forgiveness
is the understanding
that we are all affected by the forces in this life
that pull us away from a sense of wholeness
and draw us away
from our relationship with our spiritual selves.
Forgiveness
is the understanding
that our despair and trauma
impair our ability
to act in harmony with our true purpose,
which is to respect and honor life.
Forgiveness
is an act of liberating ourselves
from the spiritual prison of hate and resentment.
And it is by liberating ourselves
that we liberate others.
And it is by liberating others that we liberate ourselves.

TO THOSE I LOVE

It is very difficult to explain
what my love for you is like,
but I will try.

I will start here and hope that you understand a little more
about what I ache to tell you every minute of every day.

My love for you is like the rain falling on a lake,
a hidden romance of a being coming home to meet itself again,
an obscure window into the metaphysical eternal recurrence,
an organic representation of the beginning
that is intimately influenced by
and is the gestator of all endings.

It is like a warm wind racing across a desert,
lifting and carrying
centuries of geological sorcery
out across great distances,
silently elevating and dispersing all that has disintegrated,
and then re-focusing and re-forming—
bearing forth a new, equally powerful whole.

It is like the sound of the morning
arising from a soft whisper into a choir of life—

the physical and the spiritual opening like a blooming flower,
both still and in motion all at once.

It is like the words of a prayer that float into the atmosphere
and softly turn into the breath that someone takes in,
filling the soul with the beauty of being alive.

It is like a howling across a darkness
that spirit-speaks the words
"I am here.
Come curl yourself into the cadence of my voice
and within the walls of my heart."

It is like the wrapping of one body around another
in an act of re-creating and validating some
ancient mathematical duality—
cognizing and sacralizing the timeless child-womb relationship
that gave us our first memories of home.

It is like warmth materializing out of
hands held closely together,
allowing us to realize that any two touching objects
can spontaneously give birth to something magical,
something that cannot always be seen
but can be intensely, passionately felt.

It is like the sweet, massaging breeze
that pushes its way onto,
into,
and between
the folds of the human body during the

hottest part of any given day.
Uplifting the human chassis from a position of utter collapse
into the position of cool, somatic pride.

It is my love for you.

It is like a gravitational force
in search of and attracting all things of weight and mass,
like love—
pulling the idea and the reality
of who we are into its fields
and exploding into galaxies
in which the mind/self
can everlastingly soar.

It is a tremor in the cosmology of being
that turns the philosophical concept of
"I think, therefore I am,"
into
"I think, therefore you are
the object of my deepest affection."

It is like a single gear that has no way to turn around
without being gently, precisely, thoughtfully positioned
next to its counterpart.
Once done,
their movement together becomes cardinal to their existence;
the movement of one will not occur
in any natural way
without the other.

My love is like a geometric inversion
shaping a circle into infinity—
no matter how compressed or elongated,
no matter how brief time is on this plane,
it will never come to an end . . .
it will never come to an end.

To those I love,
To those I love,
To those I love.

HUMILITY

I will listen
as you speak,
constructing an armature of questions
that invite you to say more.

I will listen with my heart
as you unwind your thoughts
and chance to explore and expose all that you feel.

In this precious moment of mutual grace,
I will sit in the quiet of your words
and use your taking of my time
as an opportunity to give.

WHO I AM

I have no choice but to be who I am.

I am a self constructed of many selves
I am the child of Elizabeth Mae Hudson.
I am the ghost of her history
and of the history of all those
who came before her.

Still here.

I am the traces of blood spilled
upon plantation crops
and dripping down the sides of trees—
as natural as sap.

I am an old spiritual,
written and read,
sung and recited,
arising from the sweat of my ancestors,
hummed in the fields of their oppression.

I am a portrait of a people,
sculpted and painted by time itself,
made of flesh and blood

and steel and stone.
I am solid, liquid, and gas—

I am still here.

You can hold me in your hands,
drink me into your body,
or breathe me into your soul.

STILL HERE.

That is who I am.
That is simply who I am.

LOSS

The appearance of death is unpredictable,
an invasive, intrusive force,
uncontrolled
and indiscriminate.

As I watch my brother lingering in a dead zone,
a deathlike unconsciousness,
one difficult to comprehend,
I am aware that I too am lingering in death,
though conscious.
Left to examine the details of dying
in a way that only comes through this mournful,
deeply intimate affair with mortality.

MAXWELL

First your perfect hands and fingers find
themselves rustling through my hair;
your head then rests against my shoulder.
The gentleness of your palms lightly embraces
my face and pulls it closer to yours.
Your lips form a kiss; you place it on my cheek.
You squeeze me tightly, lean back,
and look into my eyes.
Your lips then form the words, "We are best friends."

Your three-year-old body is in constant motion.

You will not let go of me; your touch is what keeps us real.
Your love for me and your ceaseless, physical affection
are part of the beauty of childhood.

It is pure.

Simple.

It is real.

You slide down my body,
holding onto my hands.

You smile because you know you are safe.
I will not let you fall.
You climb back onto me,
up into my arms,
and fold me into yours,
flip around, and allow me to cradle you.
I think about how you must still remember the
nine months of being one with another.
It was not too long ago—not really.

When we are together,
it is a time for you to find your way back home
to your original motherland—
a powerful, emotional journey
back to the one place you unquestionably belonged.

We are at school.
The other children play around us;
their laughter occasionally breaks our love trance.
They giggle at our closeness.
By five or six years old,
they are already embarrassed by seeing
evidence of being "in love."

They publicly mask their need to create oneness
and instead
use me as base
in their game of tag.

They place their hands on my leg.
They press their bodies fully against mine every now and then.
"You can't tag me because I'm touching Ms. Gillette," they say.

My being becomes a magical one that
keeps them safe from the tagger.
They find their own ways to journey home—
to keep me close,
to feel my love for them,
to keep me real.

But as for you and me, Maxwell,
we are unmasked—
we are happily public about our closeness . . .
and our love for one another perfectly creates
a way for each of us
to journey back home.

NAMELESS CONVERSATION

He said,
"Only adults know true love.
It is the pain of loving
and the struggle with it
that makes it true."

She said,
"Children know true love
because it is knowing how to love truly
that makes it true.

"It is the unfaded, primal memory
of being one *with and within* another
that makes it true.

"It is the love that is instinctively accepted
and gracefully,
freely given
that makes it true.

"It is the love that sees no body type,
no age,
no skin color,
no materialism,

no barriers to loving in and of itself
that makes it true.

"It is the ability to see life for what it is
reflected in another
and then reaching out for that life through love
as if it were the warmth of the sun."

He said nothing.

She said she had always known true love.
She knew it
ever since she was a child.

Note: Bar in Brooklyn, August 24, 1995

NEW YEAR/2011

As I think about the approaching new year
and as I reflect on the time gone by,
the triumphant and the tragic,
I find myself in sorrow
for those things
that I have lost,
and thankful for what I still have.

I find myself humbled
by the perfectness and the beauty of loving
and of being loved.

As I think about the approaching new year,
I think of you.

I wish you well.

May goodness surround you—always.

REFLECTION

Let our humanity be the lens through which we view
the world around us.

Let our search for equality and justice
be the mirror through which the image of who we are,
what we hold sacred,
where we find peace,
and how we love,
be reflected onto all life.

Let us see clearly,
and let us remember
that we can only be free from hate and prejudice
by allowing others to be free.

THE BREADTH OF A TREE

The true breadth of a life
is in the joining together of many lives within one.
It is in the internal, metaphysical evolution
of the individual selves within us
merging and forming a whole.

It is a timeless process,
a human journey
in which its beauty and richness does not lie
within the smoothness of such a process
but in the challenges it brings.

It is a journey of becoming.

It can be likened to certain trees that
grow to unfathomable girth
solely because of the perfect and harmonious
convergence of separate parts into one.

Even if one of its parts is damaged
or destroyed,
still
another will rise and give power to the whole.

It is remarkable.

It is wondrous
in that any loss
automatically begins transforming into a gain.

This process is sacredly similar
to the making of the human spirit.

It is the birth of the soul.

A profound nativity,
paralleled in nature
through the coppicing
and the breadth of a tree.

SPIRITUS

Although many things

can disrupt the tranquility of a river,

nothing can keep it from moving.

OUR DIVINE PURPOSE

It is our relationship with those around us
that illuminates the darkness
and gives us light
so that who we truly are
is unobscured.

It is the community of love and companionship
that gives us a chance to hope,
to dream,
and to feel the warmth, meaning,
and prevailing purpose
of our existence.

We can see within and without more clearly
in the presence of others,
for they ignite our souls and illustrate how we are not alone
as we move along the path of our spiritual journeys.

LUCINDA

She asked me when I was coming back to see her,
her voice trembling
and her eyes squinting with sadness and sincerity.
I told her I wasn't sure, but it would be soon.
She leaned into me and hugged me
with a tightness and a passion that was familiar to me.
It was the kind of tightness and passion
that whispers, "Don't go."
The kind of tightness and passion that breaks the human heart
and leaves one feeling all alone,
suffering in a darkness that feels like a prison.

In her arms and through her eyes I felt a painful
connection. A somber, spiritual communion sparked
between our bodies. I softly pulled away,
and in doing so,
I wept.
For I realized that she reminded me of myself,
a lonely shadow of a person,
aching for someone to stay,
separated from any way of feeling complete;
a sort of prisoner, shaken and in mourning
for something more than life usually gives—
a place in which to feel free,

a feeling that we often find
within the soul of another,
but then they go.
And we are simply, painfully left alone
to mourn and hope
that when they return, they will somehow just stay.
To mourn and hope
that when they return,
we will finally, forever be set free.

BROTHER JAMES

You will remember me as a treasure—
a simple, loving piece of your life that took years
to come into being.

Are you sleeping?

I will remember you as the same.

I see you
locked in a morbid yet gentle state,
strangely still
as the light of your eyes flickers from day to day,
from moment to moment.

You look toward me,
through me,
and inside me
as I sit watchfully.

Your words gone somewhere far from here—
your silence sad and foreboding.

I see you still.
Still.
Quietly fading into something else.

I don't know this "something else,"
but I know it is you
almost completely hidden
within a process that will carry you
from this world of measured time
to a place of timelessness.

Is this you, my brother,
dying?
Or am I watching birth at a stage where most do not see it?

Do not sleep long in this process,
or too deeply;
it is where pain will find you.

Don't let it find you.
Sleep lightly as I sit by your side.
Hear me when I say that I still know you are there.

Sleep lightly
and know that someday we will awaken together,
renewed and reborn,
far away from pain.
And we will live in between birth and death,
and speak only of our longing to always meet again,
and I will sit,
once again,
by your side.

INVITATION

Come over.
Knock and I will answer.
We have people coming by.
They will sing "Happy Birthday" to Peter—
my dear Peter,
whose body is gradually separating from his spirit,
as all of our bodies will eventually do.

Dear Peter,
my love.
He is not feeling well today.

Come on by.
Knock and I will answer.

It is a day of love and celebration.

I know you have sorrows.
I know that for you each year
is another year that you want to simply, quietly tuck away.

I know you long for something to soothe you,
for something to take you back
to another place in time.

I know.

But come celebrate,
for Peter,
and I will celebrate for you.
For you—
a person like me,
trying to find peace,
trying to hold on,
trying to feel soothed in this world that creates sorrow.

I'll give you peace,
and I will soothe you.
I'll make a place for you,
if just for today.

Come over.

I'll be here to celebrate dear Peter
and to celebrate you.

COMPASSION

Compassion is the understanding
that the gift of life is beautiful
and that all life is precious and has meaning.

It is the active spiritual desire
to preserve that life
no matter to whom or to what that life belongs.

It is the understanding that the things
that pull us away from life
operate against our wholeness
and our harmony on this earth.

Compassion is the spiritual ability
to see ourselves in others
and to see others in ourselves

Compassion is a whisper
from the heavens
saying,
"I know you are there."

Compassion is a skill of the spirit
that allows us to absorb light
so that others may see themselves reflected in us
and we may see ourselves reflecting from others.

I REMEMBER YOU/THE TREE

I remember you.

You stood tall
and held hands with the sky,
reaching toward the light,
laughing and singing in the wind
and in the rain.
You breathed deeply
and filled me with the beauty of your own life.
Your great spirit passing through me,
inviting me into all that you are.

I remember you.

You who pulled despair out of me
and replaced it with hope
and made me believe
that I too would someday
stand tall and hold hands with the sky
and reach toward the light
and fill others with life.

I remember you.

You have always been with me,
strong and free.

You—
the timeless object,
watching over me
since I was a child.

You—a true mother of nature—
one that followed me throughout my own timelessness.

Long ago you held me in your arms
and taught me about strength and being free
as you stood,
always reaching for the sky
and toward the light.

I know you are still there,
still with me,
even after all these years.

I know you still understand who I am.
We have become kindred.

And even now,
long past my being a child,
you continue to be a mother to me,
still standing tall
and giving me hope.

RECURRENT SURRENDER

On one side of all awareness,
within the context of space and time,
there is what you know.
On the other side of that same awareness,
there is the unknown.

Yet it is not you who decides where to be
or where to enter or where to exit space or time itself,
or how to manipulate the awareness in order to create change.

The pull of other forces, hard to describe,
makes that decision.

But once all is decided,
you have *no* choice,
as you originally thought.

The forces will carry you wherever they may.

You have no strength to fight against them
or against the crumbling illusion of control.

A new understanding begins to take place,
an understanding you vaguely remember having before.

A surrendering.
And you simply must
let go.

Close your eyes
and fall into the unknown.

Let go.

You will then become one with awareness itself.
You will become one with space and time.

A birth and a death will occur,
collapsing like a star,
forming a black hole,
reconfiguring your internal universe.

All becomes quieter,
and you can relax your body
and your mind
because now the awareness and the
unknowing become one—
the peaceful eternity
of which you are finally a part.

A BRIEF ACCOUNT OF A LIFE
- Brian -

He lived within an emotional context
that placed him at risk of despair.

He spent his days hanging onto a shifting edge
above a make-do net
that separated him from the worst type of death—
the type that eats away at all things hopeful
and leaves the life it attaches itself to
in a lingering, agonizing state of psychic starvation.

The physical world of steady work
and financial prosperity
remained buried
far beneath the weighty consequences of
being born with too little means,
in the wrong place,
during the wrong time—
to a father
who was not really there for him
and to a mother who
was not even there for herself.

He was a casualty of an emotional war,
a victim of circumstance,
the progeny of a misconception
whose course in life
was set
long before he ever knew.

—Rest in Peace—

POET WIVES/TO MARYAM

We are not the wives of poets.
We are the wives of all those whose existences,
once autographed,
unfold more fully, more intimately—
the devoted companions of those whose
lives are deeply written
and gracefully recorded
and can be clearly read on the surface of their hearts.

We are not the wives of poets.
We are the wives of all those who move
to the sound and rhythm of language—
the true loves of those whose pulsating fingers
dance out the many versions of their stories
that lay spread across the surface of who they have come to be.

We are not the wives of poets.
We are the wives of all those who are touched into creation
by the hand of an author—
the impassioned friend of those whose thoughts
are powered by a single word
that becomes a narrative
that must be lovingly set down before us
and caressed by our eyes.

We are not the wives of poets.
We are the wives of those who whispered in our ears
that they understood why we write—
the spiritual counterpart of those who see us as scribes
and who gently open us up
so that they might comprehend the essence of the lyrist's soul.

We are not the wives of poets.
We are the wives of all those who held us in their hands
and gently turned the pages,
uncovering the scribbles of our inner worlds—
the faithful, attentive, other half of those who wanted to know
who we truly are
and so held us tenderly
and looked at us lovingly
and did not put us down until we were complete.

We are not the wives of poets.

THANK-YOU PRAYER

Thank you for each day.
Thank you for the memories and reflections
that are who I am.

Thank you for giving me the ability to endlessly think
and to boundlessly love.

Thank you for my consciousness
and for the vastness of the universe,
which serves as a mirror upon which I
can see a reflection of hope
for myself
and for all living things.

BUTTERFLY

I saw a beautiful butterfly yesterday
flying around outside the kitchen window.
It tapped lightly against the windowpane
and then rested on the sill,
rested in the heat of the sun.

I dreamt of you yesterday.
The spirit of our friendship
lightly tapping against my sleeping mind.
My love for you landed within my soul
and rested
in the warmth of my heart.

ONCE/I WAS

I was once visible.
I was seen standing in the quiet of an empty field,
dreaming of a time long ago
when I was able to catch a glimpse of who I truly was.

My image
sharpened and clarified by the penetrating gaze of another,
someone who believed I was there;
it was wonderful.

My perfect individuality
ablaze in the sun—at peace
and silhouetted against the light in the eyes of a friend.

I was once able to make sounds;
I was heard weeping in the darkness of my aloneness—
solemnly absorbed in the past,
when I knew less
and was less afraid.

My body
surrounded by the loving whispers
of someone who dared to hear me
and cared to listen.

My voice,
my words invited out of night—
echoing from the depth of the human spirit;
meaningful and poetic,
crisp and coherent,
transformed and intoned by the sweetness of a kindred soul.

I was once alive.
I was perceived and brought into this world
under the shadow of a strange hope.

A mystical being
who inconceivably witnessed her own birth.
Drawn into existence—
life pounding against the walls of my own soul,

splitting,

then merging into both mother and child—one and the same.

My thoughts
captured within a time before all consciousness
when I may have had a choice not to be;
it was incredible.

I was conceived by a loving mistake,
by the decision of someone or some two
who simply did not know
how pain-filled this birth would ultimately be.

SHE/BEAUTIFUL DANCER

She sees clearly
and hears loudly
the quiet messages
that tell her that her hair is "not right"
and her seven-year-old body is "too thick."

I hear them too.
I have heard them all my life.

These messages,
they are like bars around her soul,
around her mind,
and around her body itself.

I feel the bars.
I have been imprisoned behind them
since I was a child.

When I play music for the children,
I watch her
as she watches them
shake and move
and try out the latest steps.

They hear other messages—
messages that tell them their hair is right
and their bodies are fine.

I watch her as she stands apart,
sometimes smiling
but away from the happy wildness
that is their release.

I watch her
as she occasionally,
in very small movements,
tries to break through the bars.

I hope for her;
I have not been released.

She glances over at me, and I
tell her how wonderful she is.

I say,
"I know you're a great dancer.
I know you are."

She twists her lips sideways
and rolls her eyes away from me.

I look away
and smile at the rhythmic energy
that fills the room.

I look away
to give her a moment
to be alone with her thoughts.

She looks over at me again—
I look back.

I say, "I'm telling you,
I know you can dance up a storm."

She becomes intense and serious,
folds her arms across her chest
and says, "How do you know that?
You never saw me dance."

I say,
"I know,
because you are so beautiful,
and beautiful people
are always beautiful dancers.
That's just the way it goes.
I'm not even sure why."

Her face saddens.
Her eyes fill with tears.
She shrugs her shoulders
and turns away from me.

She watches the other children.

I say,
"I'll dance

if you do."
She looks at me
and smiles at the thought.

I say,
"Now, you know,
I'm a little old and hobbled,
so don't make fun of me."

She bursts into laughter.

I begin to move my head back and forth
and wiggle my shoulders.
I stand up from my chair
and take a few silly steps from side to side.
Her laughter escalates.

Her face saddens again.
She looks me in the eyes
and then looks away –
again.

Moments pass.

She begins to move her shoulders
in a wavelike fashion.
Her expression becomes one of focus,
not sadness.

She raises her arms
and lets them flow through the air
like a tree moving in the wind.

She slowly bends her knees,
lowers her body,
jumps up quickly,
spins around,
and begins again.

She joins the other children
in their happy wildness.
She looks at me and laughs.

I sit back down
and embrace her newly found freedom
with my smile.
She is beautiful.
She/beautiful dancer.

SOMETIMES LIFE

Sometimes

life

feels like a day

that went on too long.

IN 1965

In 1965, I was five years old.

The world was presented to me
in fragments of visuals and sounds
that came from pictures on the front of newspapers
and soft-toned, grown-up conversations
that drifted into my bedroom from the kitchen table.

The world came to me
through World War II movies,
newsreels about Vietnam,
war protests and rallies on the streets of the city,
and freedom songs
led by long-haired,
afro-sporting,
dashiki-wearing,
sandal-clad clergy members,
guitar-strapped and bouncing the words of
"We Shall Overcome" and "Kumbaya"
off the walls of church basements—
songs that rose like prayers
on the wings of our dreams
and off the breasts of our sorrows.

I was five years old.

The world came from remembering the storm of wails
and cries in November 1963
when John F. Kennedy
had his life brutally and mercilessly stolen from him.
And while our hearts were gasping for air,
and our countenances stricken with grief,
this great loss was continued by the loss of hope
and the brokenness of our spirits in April 1968
when Martin Luther King Jr. had his
life brutally stolen from him.

The world spun around in my head,
powered by poorly taught school lessons
on the subject of Black History
and long walks home weeping about Janice Chan,
who I did not know how to protect
from the onslaught of words like "chink" and "jap" and "go
back to where you came from" that flowed so easily from the
mouths of the white children that we went to school with.

I watched her cry,
and I did not know how to help her.

By the way,
I know now.

The world introduced itself to me
through an event that took place in Harlem, New York, in 1964,

in which one of my brothers was stabbed
almost to death in a race riot.

It came to me through my mother praying
for peace every moment of her life—
I know,
I heard.
I listened to her whispering those prayers
from the time she awoke in the morning
until the time she went to sleep at night.

The world was brought to me by my two eldest siblings,
whose casual affiliation
with the Black Panthers and the Five Percenters
brought 2:00-a.m. knocks on our apartment door
by police officers who were more like
the flesh-eating walking dead
than they were like humans—
those same police officers
who sicked a German shepherd on my sister and me
in Grand Central Station
and laughed at the terror on our faces
and the tears in our eyes
and the teeth-torn blouse that my mother had made for me.

In 1965, I was five years old.

The world opened its arms to me by the
solidarity of the Jews and the Blacks
who fought together and separately,
the very young and very old,

fighting for the right to be who they were.
They fought for freedom
and equality;
they fought to reclaim the dignity
that was almost completely wrung out of them
by institutional and individual systems of
thought that categorized them as inferior.

The world opened up to me by an older
Irish neighbor named Mr. Connolly,
who saw something in my mother's struggle
that warmed his heart
and created a loving bond between
them that I will never forget.
Whatever it was that he felt for her,
or about her,
or because of her,
forged a gentle friendship between them
that made each word my mother ever said
about "loving thy neighbor"
and "never judging anyone by the color of their skin"
like the deepest truth
I had ever heard.

In 1965, I was five.

The world came to me during one day
when I began to understand
the connection between the smallest of
creatures trying to survive
and those who were oppressed

engaging in the same struggle—
trying to survive.

The world came to me through a newly forming thought
that made me believe
that the continuance of life as a whole
was predicated on that struggle
and how even in 1965
it just didn't seem right that someone
would interrupt that struggle—
that anyone would take away another's right to try to survive,
which was, in my young mind,
the taking away of their right to life itself.

And somehow, even in 1965
when I was five years old,
that seemed wrong.

The world was brought to me
through the bars of zoo cages in Prospect Park
that made me feel imprisoned
because no one seemed to understand
that the true wonder of any animal
is in its being free—
to fly,
to run,
to climb,
to swim,
to swarm,
to roam,

to tease out its own destiny,
and to bring forth new life.

The world came to me in the form of a simple thought
as I stood on the hot, shadeless pavement of that zoo,
worded in this way:
"I think they want to go home."

In 1965, I was five.

The world came to me through a painful,
not fully ripened observation
that made me begin to realize
that both people and animals were enslaved by the meanness
and the selfishness of grown-ups.

I was irreparably disappointed.

I was only five.

Whatever was happening
throughout all the events that transformed my soul,
the world came to me through the weeping eyes
of those who simply wanted to peacefully embrace
the life they were given.

And no matter who or what the oppressive forces were,
and no matter what shape, color, or form that life came in,
life was not something easily given up
and should certainly never be taken away.

And there was something beautiful and
powerful about those truths
even back then
in 1965,
when I was five years old.

Note: I was born in 1960 in NYC. In a conversation with my beloved friend Maryam—who was discussing her SNCC activity in Mississippi in 1965 and the upcoming Fiftieth Year Commemoration of the Meredith March Against Fear that was led by Stokely Carmichael—it occurred to me that I was only five years old in 1965.

The title "1965" is a metaphor for the overall years of the sixties. The poem re-creates and illustrates some of the social, political, and personal events of that era that very much sculpted who I have grown to be. The events that are identified are not chronological.

June 23, 2016, 10:39 a.m.

TO MALACHI

August 24, 1981

When you are bigger,
after many moonshines
and many sunshines,
and after you become a great reader,
you will understand this poem.

An emptiness in my heart
is filled so completely
by the being of you,
my sweet little boy.

My eyes find absolute joy
dancing around the room along with your perfect child-energy.
I happily bear witness to the beauty of who you are.

An aching silently rings from within my soul
at the thought of never seeing you again.
You are moving away,
going back to your birth mother.

I find some strength
in the thought
that our love for one another

is unmovable
and our souls will forever travel as one.

I love you, dear Malachi.

We are the lights for each other
when the world seems its darkest.

I love you, dear Malachi.

And in answer to your questions:
"Yes, you can call me Mom.
And yes, we will play ball in the park."

TO DAULTON

I did not know him,
but somehow I loved him;
maybe it was simply because I understood who he was.
I felt the weight of his sorrows on the palms of my hands,
and I once saw his reflection
in my soul.

Life was hard on him
and wore him down.

Life became cold to him
and so, like disimpassioned friends,
they parted ways.

In a dream
his body was found lifeless and adrift
on the still waters of a placid lake.

In a dream
his body was brought to me on the arms of strangers,
who somehow knew
I had seen him in my soul.

I wept,
because even though I did not know him,
I understood who he was.

Even though I did not know him,
the light within him
allowed me to see him through a mirror of who I was.

Even though I did not know him,
I wanted life to come back to him
and be his friend again.

His body was brought to me,
carried on the arms of strangers,
through the silence of a still night
and placed by my feet.

I knelt beside him
and kissed his lips in honor of the sacredness of his existence.
I whispered in his ear
and asked him to see who he truly was
and as he truly was
reflected in my soul—
to see he was loved
and understood.

I kissed his lips and held one of my hands slightly above
him, and beginning from the bottom of his feet,
I slowly rolled my hand
palm up and palm down
along his body,

up to the top of his head
and back down to his heart.

I was unfolding the time before his death,
unfolding his pain,
inviting his soul to stand before the mirror of my own,
inviting his life to come back
and try again.

I kissed his lips
and he opened his eyes
and he stood up
and looked into me
and smiled
and I knew he was okay;
I felt it
within the depth of my soul.

FLY

In silence she watches the world take its turn
and prays that it passes her by.

She once touched the sun
and still carries the burn.
On the wings of her pain she will fly.

JAMEL'S FATHER

We saw him on Monday—late.
We finally found him an apartment of his own.

He loved it.

We hauled and carried the few possessions he had
down long corridors, through small doorways,
and into his new place.
It took many trips from my car
back to the building.

When it was all done,
he took a moment to look around.
He had not had a chance to view his new place
before that night.

He had been away for a long time
in a place that was not his own.

He loved it
and began to feel whole again.
He cried.

He talked about what he would do to decorate it.
I could see it in my head—all burgundy.
He loved the color burgundy.

He talked about having us over for Thanksgiving.
"I could cook up a great meal," he said.
He loved to cook.

It was a wonderful plan.

His new place was in Far Rockaway in Brooklyn.
There is a good reason that it has that name.
Jamel and I officially labeled him a new "distant relative."
He laughed.
He had a fantastic sense of humor.
He was a great laugher.

We embraced one another,
spoke words of love,
and said our good-byes.
That was the last time we saw him alive.

By eight o'clock the next morning,
he had passed away.

The changes that had come about for Russell,
his reuniting with us, his family,
the opportunity to be with his son Jamel,
to be together as two men,
as friends,
was one of his dreams—
they had been apart for many years.

His new apartment,
his plans for Thanksgiving,

our being together once again,
were all representations of hope.

But as life-altering as hope can be,
it is not life-sustaining.
His spirit was energized,
but his body was tired,
and so it passed away.

But I still have hope.

I hope that he is with friends and family even now.
I hope he can still feel the love Jamel and I have for him.
I hope that our stories in life are as successful as his—
a man who was lost and alone
then found himself
and understood more fully
the beauty of being with others.

I hope his new path is sweet and soft.
I hope we each will always remember to surround ourselves
and others with the warmth of life and laughter.
I hope that I will someday see him again.

February 2010

SONNETS

Life has been your art.
You set yourself to music.
Your days are your sonnets.

—Oscar Wilde

I don't mind claiming that I am still practicing when it comes to writing sonnets. It was not something I studied in any formal way. Like many people, I have been exposed to sonnets all my life simply through reading old works of poetry and from listening to actors recite some of the verses of Shakespeare in movies or plays. Also, metered verse is familiar to my ear from hearing poems like "The Night Before Christmas" or "The Raven."

Although there are several different styles of sonnets, I write mine using an English style like that of Edmund Spenser and William Shakespeare. Both used the traditional set of three quatrains and one couplet. Sonnets have a very distinct rhyme scheme of ABAB, CDCD, EFEF, GG; and the couplet amplifies a conclusion or a shift in emotional tone. Modern-day sonnets forego some of the strict techniques that were classic in English poetry, like the recognized sonnet of Maya Angelou called "Harlem Hopscotch," in which she moves away from the traditional meter and rhyme scheme:

> One foot down, then hop! It's hot.
> Good things for the ones that's got.
> Another jump, now to the left.
> Everybody for hisself.

> In the air, now both feet down.
> Since you black, don't stick around.
> Food is gone, the rent is due,
> Curse and cry and then jump two.

> All the people out of work,
> Hold for three, then twist and jerk.

Cross the line, they count you out.
That's what hopping's all about.

Both feet flat, the game is done.
They think I lost. I think I won.

I find sonnets challenging and a wonderful way of thinking about and shaping poetry. For me, the idea of taking large emotions and fitting them into a very limited frame without sacrificing the quality of what one wants to express is a powerful exercise for a poet, for the mind, and for the heart. I present to you four sonnets and what is referred to as an "irregular ode," simply as another way to share myself and my thoughts with you.

ODE TO A TREE

No greater gift upon the land
my eyes and heart behold.
Its beauty, its majestic stance,
bejeweled as time unfolds.

Its spirit birthed to grow and stretch
to dance beneath the sun.
Its grandeur by God's hands is sketched;
I feel our souls are one.

Oh tuck me in your leafy shade
and breathe new life for me.
Each day my soul will be remade,
my soul through you set free.

No gratitude can match your worth.
No greater gift upon this earth.

SONNET FOR THE SOUL

The seasons of my life are shapely forms
through which my soul has passed within its time.
My senses stand me right before the storm
of sights and sounds and feelings purely mine.

My soul is like the wind; it travels free
and curls itself around and through the frames.
The sound discloses my morphology,
my soul, the wind, the wind, my soul, the same.

Oh feel, oh hear the serenade I sing,
for sight cannot reveal or trap the wind.
But love can shape the melody and bring
the soul through places it has never been.

My soul intoned through seasons loved and free,
reshaping throughout time eternally.

THE SCULPTING OF A FRIENDSHIP: A SONNET FOR CEVAN

The sun awakes and waits for her to shine.
Her gentleness is envied by the earth.
She moves through painted fields of life sublime.
Promethean, with powers to rebirth.

Her timeless beauty nascent through her art.
Emerging hues that saturate her soul.
Her passions stream like ribbons from her heart.
Her passions, prismatic stories to unfold.

A moment begets a thousand years and more.
Our friendship newly sketched—a page to turn.
Our artist hands will craft an open door.
We'll watch to see what leaves and then returns.

Our departure is fortuitous and divine.
For now, we're graced to meet again in time.

ELIZABETH HOLLOMAN

Who is this exiled woman that I see
locked in behind the coldness of these bars?
Her brokenness begot her guilty plea.
A tragedy, a chronicle of scars.

Who is this lonely one that I have found
a way to understand and love somehow?
Her darkened past of hate and acts unbound,
my heart and mind should shun and disavow.

Her life beneath the sparkling, barbing wires
illuminate internal prison doors.
Her anguished, mournful heart, her dreams expired.
Her life of prayers that time with ease ignores.

This woman who I see and gently hold,
set free to live in peace inside my soul.

FORSAKEN

The night will be her blanket one more time.
But such a cover has no warmth to lend.
Her fall between the cracks her only crime.
Surrender has become her only friend.

Her eyes can see no stars up in the sky.
Her head bowed low, weighed down by fear and shame.
Her whispered prayers, a somber lullaby.
She dreams of being faceless, with no name.

Her time upon this earth a lightless tale.
No comfort comes no matter how she asks.
Her faith is worn, her spirit torn and frail.
Her destiny a truth that wears no mask.

The night becomes the tormentor revealed,
her life encased in darkness, bound and sealed.

DREAM POEMS

'Dreams are messages sent to us by guardian spirits.
that the wise one learns to listen to the messages.
to follow its wisdom.

—bell hooks

In early summer 2017, my entire life became about poetry. I became committed to publishing *The Breadth of a Tree*. I thought about the work of well-known poets, read about how to find my poetic voice, and wrote from the time I got up in the morning until I went to sleep. I had a weekly session with my poet friend Maryam about the process of writing poetry, and every conversation I had with anyone would somehow include "poetry talk."

Sometime during this poetry craze, I began to hear poems recited to me during my sleep. The first few times it happened, I was fascinated, but I did not really focus on the poems themselves once I awakened and got into the business of the day. One morning, the dream poem "Played" was whispered to me, and I decided to write it down. Although this strange way of creating poetry began happening daily over a period of several weeks, some of them were lost from memory because I did not always have the time or the emotional energy to record them. The six that I have included in this collection of poems, letters, and dreams are my favorites. Enjoy.

DREAM POEM/PLAYED

June 25, 2016

They played her that day.
They played her like an old music box—
staccato sounds breaking into her heart,
undertoned by ceaseless, haunting vibrations
that were mindful of the moans of a spirit
forever trapped in Abaddon.

They played her.

And it was at the moment she believed they truly cared,
opened herself up
and returned the care,
that they left her behind.

The moment they had a special place to go
in their fine clothes
and with their ability to pretend
that they *were*
who they *were* not, they left her.

They left her
because she had no fine clothing

or the ability to be anyone
other than who she was.

Note: This poem was recited to me in the blackness of a dream
I had between 4:35 and 4:50 a.m. No images were part of the
dream, just these words.

DREAM POEM/THE ARTISTS

June 29, 2016

They all went in different directions
to fulfill their dreams of finding a place to call home.
They were teachers and dancers,
painters and sculptors,
singers, poets,
thinkers, and dreamers.

They were given wings that lifted their
spirits and helped them to soar.

In many ways, they were a forgotten people,
perhaps even lost sometimes,
because the world they lived in
was not necessarily the world in which they truly lived.
It was not necessarily the world to which they belonged.

Their world was a world of second sight—
a world of immortal vision,
a world in which life was lived from the inside out
and not from the outside in.

The world that they lived in
was separate from the world where others lived,

and it was only by leaving
that they would begin to discover their true paths;
it was only by leaving
that they would begin to understand the real meaning of home.

Note: This poem was whispered to me on the border of being awake and asleep somewhere between 3:25 and 3:51 a.m. Only one line was added in my awake state—the line that refers to "their true paths."

DREAM POEM/BEAUTIFUL

August 3, 2016

It is like a world that you are pulled into
that rewards you with all things life-sustaining—
emotionally, spiritually, and psychically.

It is the screen on which all meaning is projected—
images of people from the past and the present,
reflections of life before birth,
smells, sights, and sounds
that make you remember why you hang on
and make you want to be fully awake and aware;
they make you want to go back
and move forward through time all at once,
to feel the endlessness of your own existence.

It is the feeling that all thought
is eternal.

It is beautiful.

It is the sunrise,
the warming light of day
wrapped around the shoulders of a dark
structure that stands tall,
and strong,
and alone.

Today it is a simple building
silhouetted by the sun,
caressed by the morning air,
swept up by my soul,
then devoured by an insatiable urge to hold on to life.

Today it is a sweet memory from my
childhood on Seventh Street—
a place where I first gazed at the moon;
it illuminated something inside me
that made me understand that living
does not stop us from dying
and that dying does not stop us from fully living.

It is the sum total of what life is worth.
It is beautiful.

It is all things reaching for one another
and finally becoming one.

There are very few words to describe it.
It is what makes you laugh
and what makes you cry,

but it is also what puts to rest all feeling
and allows room for only being.

It is incredible.

It is beautiful.

Note: Composed by me in a dream somewhere between 3:45 a.m. and 5:30 a.m.

DREAM POEM/MEANINGLESS

August 14, 2016

You come into this world,
and you fall completely in love.

You dive into the arms of those who see you as precious
and sacred; you are invited into the
hearts of those who see you
as part of their sense of wholeness.

You come here
flowing from the blood of your mother,
stamped with her dreams of reproducing herself—
she believed in the beauty and perfectness
of new life.

You come here with others,
each flowing on the currents of the same dream,
and you begin to understand more deeply
the love that brought you here,
the love you fell into
from the very moment of your birth.

You allow yourself to be held closely
within the loving hands

of those who see your worth
and who make a vow to see you clearly.

You do the same.

You look into the eyes of those around you,
cherishing that they are here with you
in this world,
and you allow them to enter into your soul.

You are attached.

You reach deep inside,
open yourself up,
and never hesitate in letting your love pour forth;
you instinctively know its true nature.
It is unstoppable.
It pours forth.

You love your home,
your family, your books, the masks you collect, your dreams,
and life itself.

You come into the world,
and you fall in love,
and that same world comes into you,
and you are even more deeply attached.

It is all so meaningful—

being part of a whole—

it is all so meaningful.

Then one day you realize
that it will all eventually fade away.
You then find
that you don't know how to feel.

You don't know what to do with all the
love and attachment.

And the world that you are in love with,
the world that you came into
and all that it meant,
becomes meaningless.

And somehow,
your love continues to pour forth,
but you simply no longer understand why.

Note: This dream came to me in sections from several flash-dreams I had somewhere between 5:30 a.m. and 6:00 a.m.

DREAM POEM/WRITTEN

August 19, 1983

She dreamt that she was a great writer
trapped somewhere between a long ago
and the time that never existed,
that never was.

She was whimsical and wise
and had everything she needed right beside her—
books, thoughts, feelings, photographs, memories, and dreams.

She wrote ceaselessly,
allowing her inner self to unfold
onto sheets of paper.

Somewhere in that long ago,
she discovered
that she herself was already written
by the hands of time,
and this made her happy.

Somewhere in that long ago,
she had become aware
that writing was her true freedom,
her way of going back in time
and returning again and again.

Note: This dream poem was found in a diary that was in an old suitcase in our apartment on Twelfth Street.

ROADSIDE DREAM POEM/CHESAPEAKE BAY

The voice of nature fell into a soft whisper
that some of us could still hear.
Some of us had heard her screaming for our attention before
but could not convince the others
to respond to her cries of "No more."
The birds and insects flew high above the clouds
and hid between the rays of the sun.
The creatures that could not fly,
the nonhuman creatures,
fell into a sleep on mountaintops
close to the stars.
The rest of us were awake and earthbound.

Most were frightened as we watched the sky darken,
and we felt the first mists of water spray upon our faces
and drip into our mouths;
it was saltish,
familiar.
It dripped into our mouths from up above.

I was not frightened and felt more awake than I ever had.
I was not frightened
because I simply understood.

Some of us fled home.
Some sat weeping in their cars.
Some stood beneath awnings close to the buildings,
huddled together on their knees,
and hoped
and prayed
that what we all thought was happening
was not.

Our hearts pounded in our chests,
and we all wept.

Some cried out
and begged the earth for forgiveness
but were not heard.

All around us we watched the streams and rivers and ocean
as they rose high against the sky,
standing tall and large like an animal making
itself bigger in the face of an enemy.

We watched the waters rise
until we could no longer keep our heads up,
and so we all bowed before it.

And in one flashing moment,
it all dropped down upon us,
crushing us,
smashing the buildings,
wrapping everything into the whorls of its power,
washing everything out of sight

until the earth was emptied of all things—
except the sleeping animals
and the birds and the insects
who had closed their eyes and hidden their faces.

And that was that.
The ocean curled itself into a fetal position
as if it were waiting to be born anew.

LETTERS

More than kisses, letters mingle souls.

—John Donne

It saddens me that I don't write letters as much anymore. It is easy to attribute this paucity to a busy work schedule and an all-absorbing focus on family and other commitments, but the truth is that my letter writing has diminished because, like any love, the object of affection begins to fade with time when unrequited. Letter writing is simply a thing of the past and is steadily dying out of our culture.

When I think about letter writing, I think of it in the context of love letters, an intimate way to communicate. They can be written to a friend, child, or family member for the sole purpose of sharing myself with someone who is beloved, letting them know how I am doing, what I am thinking, and inviting them to share with me.

There are many ways to keep in touch, and each has its place. E-mailing and texting are presently the main two. The problem with them is that they have come to almost completely replace the fundamental concept of letter writing, and somehow using them allows the writer to ignore a format that conveys any intimacy at all.

The majority of e-mails I receive, even those that are personal in nature, do not include any salutation, nor are they concluded or signed with anything more than a name. A lovely, personal valediction is quite rare. For the most part, they are written like informal business letters. Texts are even more notoriously bare of any personal touch. What I am still not used to is that once someone finishes what they want to say, they just stop texting. There is no wind-down, no warning that the communication is aborted, and no closure. I fully understand e-mails and texts as a quick way to be in touch. But in general, even when they are relatively long, they still lack the thoughtfulness and intimacy of letters.

As far back as I can remember, writing letters has always been a pleasing way to share news with people who are dear to me. Letters allow others time to hear my love for them in the quiet form of the written word without their having to immediately respond.

Letter writing is also a form of listening. When I write a letter to someone, I am listening with my heart and emotionally processing the meaning of the relationship. I write letters simply to say something that can sometimes be said more sweetly on paper. Life moves quickly, and I believe that when we focus on love, we find time to pause. Writing letters is my time to pause; it is one of the ways I express my closeness and affection in the time that I have been given on this earth.

Recently, when I was reorganizing my apartment, I uncovered a very old suitcase that had fifty to sixty diaries and journals in it dating back to 1976. I sat and flipped through many of them and found page after page of letters that I had written to various people that I knew or was beginning to know; there were letters to the teachers who were very dear to me and letters to my family and friends. I imagine that most of those letters were never copied and sent to the persons they were meant for, and they stayed tucked away in those books—the reflections and contemplations of the young, socially and emotionally solitary person I was back then. They exposed a variety of my inmost feelings, from fear to sadness to joy, all written in the context of love.

This section of *The Breadth of a Tree*, subtitled "Letters," includes love letters written in a few different styles. One or two may feel more like poems, others more like essays. Whatever form they take, they disclose some of my deepest feelings about the person to whom they are written. I hope they are inspiring—reminders of the gift that words can be, a suggestion to detail our affection toward someone, an invitation to courageously speak our love, a tender description that can help outline the closeness we feel with another. I hope you enjoy them, and I hope you experience the love they are meant to convey.

DEAR FRIEND

December 2015

Each time I speak with you,
it reminds me that my time here in this life is not in vain.
The deep love I have for you,
for your wisdom,
for your sensitivity,
for your emotional brilliance,
helps to quiet some of my aching,
because simply put,
there is something truly healing about being able to love.

I dreamt of you;
we were talking about life.
We warmly exchanged stories of how we have come to be
who we have come to be.

I dreamt of you.
The world around us slumbered.
The night was still and attentive
as it listened to our voices
purl along the strands of our time together.

I dreamt of Seattle.
It is one of those places where the natural world reaches out

and takes you passionately into its arms.
The story you told me about your experience on a reservation
there completed my endearment to it
and to you.

I wish the time we spent talking
was all there was in this world,
but that is just another dream.

Anyway, I thank you for your beauty.
I thank you for your gentle soul.
I thank you for the life you have led
that eventuated your ability to feel deeply
and to understand, in detail, how life can break the heart
but how compassion can heal the soul.
I thank you for leaving footprints of hope
as you pass through these days.

I thank you.
I thank you for making our friendship a journey of love.

peaches

DEAR PHYLLIS

January 2014

I'm afraid I'll never see you again,
but that is the way some lives go.

I once had a dream about you—not long ago.
You were dancing, funny, sweet, and playful.
Our souls were those of children again.
We were in love with life—
and it made us laugh.

You danced.
One step forward, two steps back,
rock to the side, bow and slide.
We were happy.

We have not spoken for years.
We have not seen one another since Russell passed along.
His passing—
a reminder of our own funeral—
our relationship long departed,
a death that is quietly masked,
unspoken of
but true.

We have not loved or laughed for decades.
Our romance of a life together
passed along.

It occurred to me as I awoke from the dream,
while lying in the shadow of a slow sunrise,
that we were lost from one another some
time back when we were young.
I somehow became something you would grow to hate.
I think this fate was born before we were,
perhaps even before our own mother's birth.

Perhaps in another life we'll meet again—
perhaps even as the sisters we are.

I hope.

And I hope we will be,
even then,
aware that we knew one another.
And even then
we will apologize
for ever forgetting how to love
and dance
and laugh.

Perhaps we will begin to feel that same
pounding of our hearts—
a music that belongs just to us.
It will be a tribute to the old and the new,
a perpetual rebirth.

Perhaps we will have a better chance of staying together,
a better chance of never getting lost.
Another chance to be
the dream I once had.

Love, peaches

THANK YOU, JAMES

June 2016

Thank you, James,
for being with me today.

Your presence was deeply felt,
and it allowed me emotional access to something I rarely feel—
a sense of home.

I imagine that part of this feeling came from the
fullness of love that I knew was surrounding me—
I felt complete.

Another part of this feeling came from witnessing your
excitement over the success of Saturday's work,
and then, later that evening,
the same feeling ran through my soul from listening
to you reflect on your initial doubt about whether or
not the activity that I was doing with the children
would unfold smoothly or favorably enough
to be what you wanted to capture on film.

I was hypnotized by your energy,
drawn into your passion,

inspirited and touched in a different way
by your flawless humanness.

The last two days with you and Jenny
filled me with happiness.
I felt as if life had renewed itself.

And even though the days have passed
and you are gone
and the energy that soared around us
is in the process of being swept away on the tailcoat of time,
it will stay in my heart.

Thank you, James.

Although the purpose of our being together these past
days was related to our work on the documentary,
I experienced a beautiful shift in our friendship—
a shift that can be equated to adjusting an article of clothing
to a position of perfect comfort.

Thank you, James.

I look forward to seeing you again.

Love and peace to you always,

Your friend,

peaches

DEAR JAMEL

May 2011

I stand before a painting here at the Rubin Museum called the *Mandala Shambhala.* It is a painting of a world. Some of the images of this world are distinct and clear, some are faded and obscured, but everyone and everything in it has a place. This painted world displays layers of life and the business of the living.

I stand before it pensively, curiously, enviously staring at the perfect details of the depicted lives—those in prayer, meditation, and in battle. I feel as though those who occupy this world are staring back at me. I first approached it thinking I would somehow translate it, a required part of a writing assignment, but it cleverly and quietly translated me.

The world of the *Mandala Shambhala* is the framework around an existence that is made up of many existences. It deeply reminds me of how the whole and its parts are eternally woven together. It deeply reminds me of how each of us, in the grand scheme of life, is the translator and the translation.

Within this world, oldness and newness are both represented on a continuum, a reminder that history cannot be separated from the present or from the future—a reminder of you and me. The stories of our lives act as a moving force that interacts with and

121

influences what will become the past, what is now the present, and what will be the future—each one continuously confronting the other.

Although you did not come into this world through my body, we are eternally woven together by a fate that placed us in our own world, one in which I became your mother and you, my child. This perfect relationship came into being by a sweeping wind produced in the bowels of something holy and carried on the breath of prayers and meditations—whispered into birth through our own Mandala Shambhala. Our togetherness was translated by something divine. Through the blood of my brother, your father, we shared a history, shared a spiritual past, and shared a present and a future.

Our incarnate connection began long, long ago—our mutuality detailing our own history that folded quietly into the present and then into the future—our timeless kinship respiring through our blood and our bodies and creating an eternal affinity.

I never wanted to have children. I was always afraid that they would be like me—a being washed in sadness and heartache that has followed her through a million lifetimes. But somehow, when the opportunity came to take you in, to remove you from the hands of the dark matriarch whose body you did come through, the one ironically brave enough to have children, I did not hesitate.

She could not see you clearly. She could not translate your world enough to be able to see the beauty of your being, of your life. I see it. I see you clearly—I see your beauty. I always have, and I always will.

We have both witnessed and created the details of our lives together, using our history to frame our present and to diagram our future. We have a place in this world. We are the whole and its parts; we are the translators and the translated. We have been composed by a past that no one can un-compose. We are a moving force, a holy breath, the focus of the meditation of a god. We are life itself. You and I, Jamel—our time on this earth layered and folded together throughout all these years, embraced by the old and the new and wrapped up by the past, the present, and the future.

We stand before one another, and like the *Mandala Shambhala*, we depict a world—our kinship perfect and immortal, our souls eternally woven together, our lives beautifully layered and painted with love.

You and I, Jamel.

You and I.

TO JENNY

Today/June 2016

There are times when I am so enamored with
someone's spiritual beauty,
with their bodiless selfhood,
with their emotionally, alluring individuality,
that I don't readily see their physical being;
it appears to me as an afterimage of sorts.

It was only as I viewed you retrospectively,
within the range of vision that memory permits,
that I perceived how beautiful you looked today.

The pinkness of your blouse
delicately sleeping against your skin.
Your hair pulled back, awakening your perfect face,
your radiant voice reaching out,
inviting others into the sound of your laughter—
allowing me to regress back to a time
wherein life felt safe
and going home was not just a dream.

You looked beautiful today.

Both your interior and exterior selves move gently,
filling the room like air
and taking part in giving life,
procreating
a series of sublime moments.

Today.

I am glad I saw you.
I am glad I saw you today.

Your soul, your body,
your spirit, your soul,

each beautifully visible,

each distinctly manifest.

Today.

TO MARYAM FROM PEACHES

July 10, 2016

It's interesting. Right?
The energy force that is us,
that is the genesis of our being, especially as poets.
We, by our nature, have strange spirits
that spread across the universe,
traversing many dimensions,
and so we often seem as if we are not here,
not grounded in the way that others can understand.

It is sometimes a struggle.
We can awaken at any given time and not
know where we are for a moment,
or even what state of mind we will be called to exist in,
or what condition our heart is in—tender or strong—
or what mind we will wander through
for the time being.

Sometimes we are focused and energized,
efficient and comprehensible.
Sometimes we are gloomy and unclear,
silent and lost in our own dreams—awake or asleep.

(Or maybe we are actually someone else's dream.)

In any case,
this is the mind of our poet selves.
It is interesting.
I'll talk to you soon.

Note: Post–Poetry Session. Shared Google Docs Letter, 9:30 a.m.

DREAMS

Who looks outside, dreams;
Who looks inside, awakes.

—Carl Gustav Jung

Transcribing a dream can be very intense in that I must stay focused on every aspect of the dream immediately upon awakening, with book and pen nearby. Concentrating on each detail—the visual and emotional texture, the pace, who the characters are and what they represent, and the shifts in time and place itself—is the only way to reconstruct this sleep-world with authenticity. Every motion or even a deep-enough breath can sometimes send my memory of a dream scattering into the ether—disintegrating its whole and leaving me with disconnected parts never to be integrated again.

Equally as intense as transcribing dreams is putting together a narrative that allows the reader to absorb its meaning enough to appreciate some of the more personal, nonuniversal symbolism. Transcribing dreams is the elaborate task of turning something that is abstract into something that is concrete.

Dreams are interesting, and the world of dreams is fascinating. In general, when reading a transcribed dream, the reader must understand two very important things: First, dreams have no way of conforming to standards of time and place or to reality as we know it in the waking world. Second, in my dreams, there are times when I am simply an observer, times when I am a participant, and times when I switch back and forth. Additionally, while I am dreaming, I commonly fall into a trancelike state or momentarily fall into a secondary dream.

Although most of my dreams are laced with clarity and can be written down accurately, there are times when I need to fill in a few details in the same way I sometimes do with dream poems; dreams do not always give me images to work with; some of what I experience comes in the form of feelings that are not observable in any way; I then need to find the right words to translate what was felt. In the dream "Matra and Joff," I filled in some of the details of their "physical" world. In the dream poem "Played," someone whispered the word "abado." It took a little research and an educated guess to conclude that it was "Abaddon."

Often, someone I know well in my awake life will appear in the form of someone or something else. I feel who they are, but I do not see them as who they are in reality. In some of my dreams, I knowingly meet myself. Sometimes I am who I am outside of the dream, and sometimes I am in another form, such as light or wind.

I love my dreams. I love the process of dreaming. I love thinking about my dreams, and I love writing them down. They help me unearth deep thoughts about the world and about my past experiences. At the same time, they fulfill a personal yearning that allows me to go back home or to meet family members who have passed away.

The dreams that I have included in this book are my favorites for several reasons:

1. They happen in a place or dimension that represents my childhood home on Seventh Street.
2. I am aware that I am dreaming.
3. My role in the dreams allows me to switch between observer and participant.

4. The symbolism is obscure and creates the opportunity for me to be a detective of my own thoughts and feelings, which I find exhilarating and rewarding.
5. I am aware, even in the dreams, that I encountered myself.
6. The pace of the dreams is slow, and the sequence of events is clear.

Dreams are a powerful, emotional world in which some of my many selves can be freely expressed. I find them to be magical and profound; they are a landscape of endless possibilities. I hope they inspire you to look at your dreams through a new lens and to perhaps write them down.

DREAM OF BROTHER JAMES

July 6, 2016
Between 2:45 and 3:10 a.m.

There was something perfect about the way the air felt on my skin—something about the sound of the wind passing through my loosely fitted blouse, the color of the sky, and the snow that gently fell that gave me a feeling of warmth. It was good to be home, standing on the front stoop of my childhood apartment building on Seventh Street. I was happy, and it made me smile.

My mother's energy moved within me with every breath I took. Visions of her face—the mirror image of my oldest brother's face—floated like a sweet ghost before my eyes and made me weep deep inside. I stood on the stoop of my home on Seventh Street and faced east toward Prospect Park. It seemed that all meaningful movement in Park Slope came from the east. It was the direction of the major bus lines and subways, the major shops and restaurants, the neighborhood hospital, and Prospect Park. The park was one of the most emotionally significant places of my entire life; it was where I found great freedom as a child. The first place I found that freedom was in my home on Seventh Street.

As I stood on my stoop with my eyes fixed on the falling snow and on the trees that still had their leaves, I fell into a trance—into an inner world where a second dream took place, a dream about playing with my brothers and my sister in our backyard. We were tumbling around in the leaves, tickling one another and laughing. Our laughter quieted into smiles as our eyes focused on a beautiful white butterfly. We watched it, fascinated by its large wings and its movement through the air. When I came out of the trance, still standing on my stoop, I found myself gazing east toward the park, aware that I was waiting for someone to come. I was not sure who it was, but I knew it was someone I loved and ached to see again, someone I had not seen in a very long time. I was excited. I felt like a child watching the first snowfall of the season.

There is something simply magical about snow falling that only a child understands; it is a magic that lifts you up and transports you into a state of bliss and wonder. It is a magic that grabs your attention and mesmerizes you, and no matter how still you are, if you stare into the snow as it falls, you begin to feel that you are moving with it—like the emotional movement that comes with the yearning to go back to an earlier age. No matter how still the past, no matter how fixed in space or time, if you stare deeply enough into it, you begin to feel that you and the past are moving together.

I stood with my eyes slightly closed, a smile softly resting on my face. The snow had begun to whip around wildly, almost like the flight of a butterfly. I saw a figure moving toward me from the east but still far enough away that I could not tell who it was.

As the figure got closer, I noticed a vaguely familiar grin revealing itself from under a large, baggy hood and from between the corners of an upturned coat collar. The figure, a man, was moving briskly, youthfully, and confidently. Each step he took was strong and assertive, as if the world had been placed under his feet just for him. As I watched his movement toward the building, I had the strong sense that he knew I was waiting for him.

He lifted his face slightly upward, not enough for me to see it fully but enough to allow me to know that it was a familiar one. My mind began scanning through possibilities; perhaps it was an old schoolmate or a former neighbor. I simply did not know. I closed my eyes and fell into a second trance.

In this trance, I was a young girl, about nine or ten years old. I was watching the neighborhood boys playing stickball in front of the house. I was smiling but was flooded with sadness—the feeling was overwhelming. I felt a sharp pain inside, clutched my stomach, and doubled over; someone was missing and it made me ache. I began to cry and then watched all the boys fade away. When I came out of the trance, the approaching figure was just a few feet away from the gate of the building, standing still and smiling. I knew with certainty this person was someone I loved deeply, someone I wanted to talk to. I felt I had a world of things to say to him. I imagined us sitting together on the stoop, talking for hours and remembering people we knew and movies we had seen together. We would grin as we shared memories of the taste and smell of my mother's biscuits or memories of her dog—an overactive, white German shepherd that would run away every chance it got but always returned home. I realized that we knew one another in a special way; this man was no schoolmate or neighbor. He was someone else.

He stepped through the gate, and as he did, he lowered his collar and slowly slid back his hood, and I saw it was my brother, my brother James. His smile was wide: it was the kind of smile that holds back a laugh until the right moment. I had not seen him in such a long time. We were the bookends of our family, he was the oldest child, and I, the youngest. We had twenty-three years between us, and sometimes he felt like a stranger to me, but our love for one another was something quite familiar.

As he began to walk up the steps toward me, the snow sparkled around him. My heart filled with joy, and my thoughts swirled with plans to catch up on all the time we had lost. As I opened my arms to embrace him, I heard my mother's voice from behind me saying softly, almost in a whisper, "You know, it's not the season for this." And then there was silence, and everything faded away: first my brother, then the snow, then my home on Seventh Street, and then the dream.

Note: My mother passed away when I was twenty-one. It saddens me that I never had the chance to know her as I matured into adulthood. She was the center of our family universe, and her death created a black hole that sent each of us scattering and lost in a world that no longer felt like home.

For many years, James and I were separated. Our age difference placed us on very different paths at completely different times. Through my mother's stories, I was aware that he lived a difficult life, haunted by memories of growing up in harsh conditions of racism and poverty in Maryland, where he was born in 1937.

Through a series of life circumstances, we reconnected. We were able to internalize and apply our mother's lessons about love, compassion, and the specialness of family. James and I became dear friends. We laughed a lot, and he shared stories of our mother's history and of his life as a child—a life he and she made for themselves long before I was born. We developed a bond that was unique. There was nothing we would not do for one another, and we never separated again.

In his later years, James became very ill and had both legs amputated; he lived out the rest of his life in a wheelchair. He struggled with heart and kidney problems and bouts of depression. He passed away in hospice approximately one year ago. His death was emotionally dissolving for me, not only because of his physical resemblance to my mother but because of the deeply loving relationship we had come to have. He was my brother. I miss him, and I hope we meet again.

SEAR
1978

She was a wonderful child, full of life. She was always planning to change the world, and while she was at it, she planned on making some changes in herself as well. She was poor of material possessions but rich in the belief that life was good and could be made better with a little faith and a little work.

She was about nine or ten, according to this dream, and she spent all her time actively engaged in life through her hopes and fantasies, and by talking to everyone she met about her big and wonderful ideas—she was going to save the world and build a rocket that would one day take her far away. As she would often say, "It isn't always good to stay in one place for too long."

She played outside all day, every day in front of her home on Seventh Street, and that was her life; it was like a beautiful dream. The days were always warm and shiny, and happiness spilled from her heart onto everyone she met and was returned to her through their love and their smiles. Well, this was the case in relation to everyone she met, with one exception. He was known in the neighborhood as Sear. Everyone knew who he was, and everyone shuddered when they heard his name, shuddered when they heard his voice . . . ran and hid when they heard his thundering footsteps coming near.

She had seen him only once before, when she was younger. She remembered looking into his eyes, ready to smile and welcome him into her heart. She remembered looking into his eyes and seeing nothing, feeling a charge of something so dark coming from within him that she had to look away, to run away and hide until the feeling passed. Even the thought of him was enough to frighten her.

He was a very large man in every way, and his heart was cold and hard. He saw only the flaws in the world and did not care how much everyone feared him or even hated him, because he himself hated everyone, with no exception. He hated absolutely everyone, and he hated everything. He had no dreams of any kind, and so he had no way to rearrange his perception of life. He did not see beauty in anything; he hated life, he hated "dreamers," he hated hope, and he hated her as she flitted around the neighborhood with her endless good cheer and her thoughts of a better world.

Life to him was like the "devil's joke," he once said. "Life as a Black man was cruel and hopeless. Life for all Black folks was bad and would always be bad. Life was a twisted, deformed thing that should be put out of its misery."

Everyone knew he had a special hate for her. He hated her mountain-brown skin and her stupid ideas, her happy way and her ridiculous dreams; he hated her belief that if you allowed your heart and soul to guide you and to do your talking and playing and dreaming for you, life could only feel good. And it did not matter what color your skin was because the true human spirit had no particular color; she believed this with all her heart. Well, he did not believe this in any way at all. What he believed was that the world was full of Satan's murderous creations that were against Black folks, and those who did not see this should be beaten and hollered down until they did see it or until they themselves did not exist any longer. They needed to see the truth, he believed—she needed to see the truth.

Everyone on Seventh Street was afraid of him. He walked the blocks of the neighborhood shouting hatred—shooting hatred from his eyes and mouth as if they were bullets from a gun. He told people what to do and when to do it. He told them what to think and when to think it, and they obeyed.

In her world of dreams and happiness, the reality of who he was never entered her mind. She was busy. She played with whoever she wanted and did whatever she liked. She had tea parties in front of her house and invited everyone to attend; she carried pockets full of change she had earned by selling small wishes and used the change to buy more tea. She believed that one should always be prepared for spontaneous adventures, and so she carried maps of the stars because she knew that it would not be long until she built her rocket.

One day she heard a rumor circulating on Seventh Street that he felt it was time to stop her nonsense. He said the time had come to beat the truth into her and finally put an end to her lies and to her life itself if that's what it took. He felt she was poisoning the minds of too many. He felt that she needed all the silly dreams and thoughts of racial harmony and the blatant defiance of his ways beaten right out of her. Didn't she know that black or brown skin would always be the markings of inevitable failure? Didn't she know that he was tired of her incessant playing and dreaming? Didn't she know that she was Black, was as brown as a mountain and had no right to feel happy or to dream?

Yes. She heard about the rumor, heard it so much that the reality of who he was began pounding in her heart. She was worried, and her happiness began to give way to fear and sadness— something she had never experienced before. She found herself all alone on the stoop of her house on Seventh Street, sitting and wringing her hands. The days lost their shine and her dreams were beginning to fade. She sat for a long time worrying and waiting for him to come. The longer she waited, the unhappier she became, and it seemed that she waited a very long time.

One day, as she sat worrying and waiting, she realized that her unhappiness had somehow turned into anger. She couldn't believe that *anyone* would want to stop her from playing and dreaming and loving and building her rocket. She couldn't believe that he wanted to stop her from making the world a better place. She felt her fear and worry being slowly replaced with the determination to continue on her mission to change the world—to play, to dream, and to love—and so she decided not to wait for him to come and find her. Then, suddenly, she saw him storming down Seventh Street a short distance away, waving his arms and yelling wildly into the air. He did not notice her until she stepped right in front of him, and when she did, she told him straight out that he was wrong about everything he felt. She told him that she did not believe in him and she did not believe in his hate. She went on to tell him that he did not exist in her world, and for her, he was like a nightmare, and nightmares had to come to an end. So, on that day, with the sun shining down on her mountain-brown skin and her spirit shining up, she hollered him down. She hollered about all the things he was wrong about—everything he did or said that promoted hate. She hollered about how happiness is real and how it means something, how life can feel right and that dreams of a better world make perfect sense and can come true. She hollered him down without taking one single breath, and on that day, Sear closed his mouth and faded away and was never seen again.

Note: I grew up on Seventh Street in Park Slope, Brooklyn. Most of my life there, particularly during the sixties, seventies, and eighties, the racial tension in the neighborhood was high and was a constant source of conflict within the entire community.

I was a whimsical child and a dreamer caught between the painful reality of racism and the desire to escape that reality.

In this dream, I am all the characters. Although my mother is not actually present, she shows up in some of the language and behavior in the dream. For example, the use of the word "holler" was my mother speaking; the belief that life was good and that no one should be judged by their skin color—those were my mother's words. The hand wringing and worry and the courage to confront ugliness and try to change it through action and faith—those were all part of my mother's qualities. Sear represented many things: the racial climate of the times as well as the self-hate and anger that was part of experiencing racial oppression and social marginalization.

MATRA AND JOFF
1998

Their love was a love so unique that it held the world in a trancelike state, a state of awe and curiosity. It was the kind of love that passes through the flesh and settles into the soul. It was a love that existed like a ghost or an apparition—clearly there but somehow untouchable—and like their love, they too existed like ghosts.

They had no knowledge of how they met or exactly when or where; they simply had no memory of it. They once explored the thought that they may have met at a concert or some type of public event, but they did not spend much time thinking about it because they didn't really care. They had no idea what era they were in; their existence felt timeless. They never wondered about what the future held for them or what they did not have; they simply created everything they needed whenever they thought of it. What they cared about was the love they had for one another and being able to bring joy to the world.

He had great vision and the mind and hands of an artist or craftsman, but his true calling was writing—spinning out stories, dreams, poems, ideas, and inventions that he would write down as he sat at his desk during the late hours of the night. She loved to sing and dance—her body a human instrument. She, too, was good with her hands; she built stages wherever she went and put on magnificent performances.

It was the magic of their qualities and the uniqueness of the love that existed between them that inspirited them, that made them happy. In many ways, their love kept them separated from the world around them. For the most part, they existed only in the minds of one another and in the mind of the dreamer. Their names were Matra and Joff.

Their desire to make others happy was one of the main reasons they visited the commons of the small, dateless town not too far from where they spent most of their time. They knew that people came from miles around and gathered just to see them, to witness their bliss, to watch them create, to hear him read his works, to listen to her voice and watch her body move and flow like the waters of the ocean. They were dearly loved. They were sent money from all over the world and received letters from admirers pleading with them to share their gifts, inviting them to live with perfect strangers. There were letters asking for advice and help, asking for things of which they had no knowledge—medical needs were begged to be met, spiritual guidance was asked to be given, help with finding true love was requested from those whose lives felt lonely. All this attention, want, and need was generated in the hearts of those who simply knew about their love for one another. Children flocked around them like birds around bread. Everyone flocked around them like birds around bread and would take in their endless, joyful energy and become contentedly full. Matra and Joff were pleased.

I, the dreamer, watched Matra and Joff live out their lives within their magical world, and I felt happy. Their endless creativity and the power of their life force made me want to be with them all the time and hold them forever in my dreams. I, too, was in awe.

Matra and Joff spent each morning of their lives together talking quietly in their room. They were the only tenants in a quaint apartment building that sat at the edge of town; no one ever entered it or visited. It was a place only for them. In fact, Matra and Joff no longer existed in the minds of the people once they left the commons for the evening, but as soon as they returned or even ventured to take short strolls out into the town, they were instantly surrounded by people of all ages who would ask them questions and tell their own stories. In a way, the people attached their lives to the lives of Matra and Joff, who did not mind. They sang and danced, and responded to every question they were asked with poems, songs, exhibitions, and unusual philosophies about the art of living.

Once, Joff theatrically announced the following thought to a large crowd: "Only by letting go of life could you truly live." The dreamer and the people did not know what Joff meant, but they loved his words, affirmed them to one another, and responded with applause and tears. As often as one could hear laughter arising from the town square, one could just as easily hear crying and weeping. Joff's words filled everyone with emotions that touched every part of their hearts.

Matra was simply enchanting: her voice rang out like the voice of an angel, and her movement was delicate and aerial. After each time she and Joff engaged with their fans—who they really considered to be their spiritual friends—the people kissed them and then fell asleep. Matra and Joff faded away along with the end of each day. Their lives were as flawless as could be. Both their world on the commons, where they could be seen and touched, and their world alone in their apartment felt perfect. Unfortunately, they were not aware of an imperfection that secretly and quietly lurked within the town, and at first neither was the dreamer.

Somewhere long into the dream, Matra's sister materialized. Her sister was married to Joff's brother. They despised Matra and Joff and loathed their undying love for one another and their spectral beauty; they sneered at their clothes, the smiles on their faces, and their happiness. They hated everything anyone can hate about another. They hated Matra and Joff's talents and were repulsed by the way others loved them; that hate eventually mutated into a nightmare that would forever change the lives of Matra and Joff.

Many mornings began with Matra and Joff pretending they were being pursued by what they called "baggers." Baggers were gentle monsters who captured and tickled them until they collapsed while pleading "No more." The pleas had to be repeated exactly seven times, and then the baggers would show mercy by setting them free. Matra and Joff, like children, played this way for hours. They would run hand-in-hand around the entire town. They could be seen, but no one spoke with them when they were playing their game of run and chase. Everyone knew that this was one of the most private parts of Matra and Joff's lives and of their love. The whole world knew that the times Matra and Joff spent exclusively with one another was the most special part of their abiding courtship. After each game with the baggers, Matra and Joff would vow to never leave one another even for a moment—and the truth was, they never did.

During one particular morning, Matra and Joff's play seemed more special than ever, and it was during this time that they decided they would move from their quaint apartment and the small, dateless town and live in a bigger part of the world so that their love could be shared with even more people and the joy that they brought could be spread more widely. Matra and Joff did not go into town or visit the commons that day; shortly after their game, they retired to their home and immediately fell asleep in one another's arms and dreamt of laughter and warm breezes that would kiss their lips and make them smile; they also dreamt of other worlds in which they would sing and build and share their happiness. These were their simple dreams, which lasted throughout the night, and the nights always felt long and splendid.

On the following morning, they were awakened by the light of the sun that spilled into their room and landed on the lids of their eyes, which opened softly. Gazing at one another, they smiled, and as their smiles curved to completion, they heard something they had never heard before—a knock on their door, which they ignored. They continued to lie together, feeling especially content with the idea of going abroad.

It seemed as though a long time had passed when Matra and Joff heard strange, fast-paced whispering from out in the hallway of their apartment. Before they could turn away from one another to try to figure out this new reality of someone, anyone, being in their private world, the door was violently pushed open. Appearing at the foot of their bed stood Joff's brother. Both Matra and Joff were stricken with confusion. Joff's brother lunged at Joff, took ahold of his sleeping gown, tore it off, and with monstrous strength, tossed Joff down a flight of stairs and into the empty street, and then he faded away. Matra's sister entered the room and began destroying all Matra and Joff's possessions. Matra sat frozen on the bed, horrified, as her sister destroyed Joff's tools, books, and papers as well as Matra's instruments and music sheets. She ripped and tore at Matra's clothing that hung in the closet and turned to Matra and looked at her with deadly eyes. Matra recoiled. Her sister reached out and wrapped her hands around Matra's throat and began to squeeze with a hate that even the dreamer could not explain. Matra's sister was shaking with rage and began to scream: "You are a witch, Matra. All your charm, your freedom, your happiness, your love—all witchery. We hate you. We hate both of you." Matra's body began to wilt within the grip of her sister's hands, and her eyes filled with terror as her mind slowly went blank. Her body became limp, and her life slowly moved away from her as if it were a departing ghost. Outside, Joff felt Matra's spirit pass through his soul; he felt her transitioning from life into death and then felt a darkness. His screams could be heard throughout the world, and the world began to weep as Matra and Joff's dream life came to its end along with the sleep of the dreamer.

THE FORFEITURE

Undated Dream

There were five of them in all, including the dreamer. They found themselves wandering across the vastness of a great desert. They were frightened and had only a bleary recollection of how they came to be where they were. They shared one memory about it—that of crawling up through a hole somewhere in the middle of the vastness, but that was all. The dreamer's sister was there along with two unknown males and one unknown female. They were thrown together in this dream from an experience the dreamer had at a workshop during her awake life.

The smell of saltwater permeated the air; it was strong, and for the dreamer, it brought memories of playing on a beach when she was a child. The memories were soft but faint because her thoughts greatly focused on her dream-mates and the portentous situation they were in.

They were exhausted and afraid, their bodies hot and aching. The feeling of hopelessness overwhelmed their minds. They found themselves in mental anguish over the fact that they had been wandering for such a long time. Their hearts weighed heavily in their chests as they dragged along, trying to find anything at all that might provide shelter or a place to rest—perhaps a building, a tree, or even a hole like the one through which they had originally crawled.

Their tired and stinging eyes painfully scanned the surface of the sand. They walked in silence, each hoping that the hole they had originally come through would appear and guide them— likening itself to a North Star—though they feared the worst, and somehow the worst was not necessarily their seemingly endless wandering. It was the feeling of being eternally condemned within a state of singular consciousness that did not allow anyone to separate his or her own fears and exhaustion from the others'. This shared consciousness only intensified what they each felt: the trauma and heartrending search for something that might never be found. Their anxiety was escalating with each passing moment; their heads were pounding with pain, their hands were shaking, their thoughts firing blame back and forth about whose fault it was that they were there. They were desperate and angry, heading toward a point of emotional collapse.

They started to feel faint, and their bodies began to slump and slowly sink onto the hot sand. They caught a glimpse of something in the distance, something more than the blinding, unrelenting particles of light reflecting off the surface of the sand. What they glimpsed was pitch-black and circular. *Oh God,* they thought. *Could this be our way back, our exit from this cruel and empty reality?* The excitement of possibly finding a way out of their nightmare, away from the torturous idea of wandering forever, lifted their hopes and their bodies. They moved hastily across the sand toward the blackness, and as they drew nearer, they fell to their knees, ready to begin their evacuation. A deep orange grating appeared, covering the hole. Its rim was securely buried beneath the sand. They frantically began to dig. They agreed that whatever fate lay inside had to be better than what they had experienced up to this point.

Tears streamed down their faces as they continued to dig, and finally, with great collective force, they managed to remove the orange grating. They laughed, tears still streaming from their eyes. They began to push at one another, fighting over who should enter first. They bickered over who deserved to enter first, and as their bickering trailed into silence, they fell into a sleep in which they were aware that they were falling through a darkness. The dreamer was aware that her sister had vanished. Only the dreamer, the woman, and the two males were left, and when their falling came to an end, they found themselves standing in what appeared to be the base of an enormous vessel. It was an old ship made of wood; it was moldy, weather-beaten, and splintered. There was something strange about it, something indescribable.

The dreamer found herself alone, standing at the bottom of a very long, broad flight of stairs. As she looked along the walls enclosing the staircase, she noticed that they were covered with strange and scary pictures—some hand drawings, some photographs. They were pictures of seamen, each with several missing body parts. In some of them, the seamen were grossly deformed and propped up against the insides of strange half-boats that were sun-bleached and deteriorated, and sets of unusually thin oars protruded from the boats. The seamen were smiling, but their smiles were bizarre; they did not represent contentment or happiness. They were sad smiles that represented surrender.

As she stood staring at the pictures, she began to tremble. She felt the terrifying presence of a monster and then fell into a brief sleep and dreamt that some faceless thing plunged a sword into her stomach and out through her back. Blood poured through her fingers as she covered the wound with her hands. When she awoke, she heard voices behind her; she turned and saw the same people from the pictures milling about—hobbling and crawling around her. Across the vessel, she saw her sister, also surrounded by the same hideous seamen. The expression on her sister's face was one of horror, and she was screaming and crying. The dreamer felt a deep pain in her heart. She wanted to get her sister away from these horrible things. The dreamer closed her eyes and wished her sister away; her sister vanished as if she were never there.

The dreamer's attention returned to the wide, long staircase; slowly descending from the very top was a man wearing a long gray robe tied with a yellow rope. He welcomed the dreamer in a way that did not feel right, a way that seemed absolutely crazy, for why would anyone feel welcome inside such a horrible place? He announced that a game was about to begin and that there were only two outcomes: The winners would receive a set of oars and a half-boat, which would be freely hoisted up and placed into a dark tunnel that would be their new home. The losers would receive no boat, no oars, and no assistance; they would have to walk into the tunnel on their own.

Somehow she knew what awaited both the winners and the losers once they entered the tunnel. In her mind, she saw a huge beast there, partially cloaked by the darkness; it was evil and depraved. It was surrounded by blood and body parts floating in waste—the remains of all those who had entered, all those who had lost, and all those who had won. Those who survived the walk into the tunnel were left mangled, flesh-shredded, and deformed, and were forced to repeat the game throughout eternity. She did not want to play. She did not want to be there; she tried but could not wish herself away like she had done for her sister. The dreamer began frantically looking around for a way out of the vessel, out of this hell. She raced up the stairs, screaming, objecting to the game, praying for another reality that she might fall into, like the hole in the desert that brought her here.

The man who made the announcement appeared by her side and put his arm around her as if to comfort her. In a soft but eerie tone, he said, "Now. Now. You all must play. Come. I'll show you how easy it is." He handed her a stack of paper money with pictures of the same deformed seamen on the front of each bill. An old desk appeared before her. Its surface looked like a cash drawer with several openings. She noticed that the openings were smaller than the bills she had been given. He placed one hand on her shoulder, and as he pulled her away from the desk, he said, "All you have to do is stand here and toss the bills so they land in any of the openings, any at all. You can do them one at a time or all at once. It never matters which way you do it." He turned and faded away.

The dreamer stared at the cash drawer and then the money. She kept wondering if it would be possible to get all the bills into the openings in one throw. He did mention that there were winners, so it must be possible, she thought. She began straightening the bills, making sure that each one was aligned with the next. Her heart was racing. *Is this possible? Could there be some magic in this?* She closed her eyes and visualized the money landing perfectly but realized again how crazy it all was. *There was no win. There were no winners in this bizarre game.*

The dreamer steadied her hands and body and again focused her eyes on the money and then on the cash drawer. She pulled her arm back slightly, tossed all of the bills at once, and watched them flutter and land on the floor. She fell to her knees and quickly gathered the money back together. She nervously stacked and straightened the bills and pretended she had never made the attempt. The announcer reappeared beside her, and in that same soft and eerie tone, he said, "Oh. I see you've missed the cash drawer." The dreamer quickly told him that he was mistaken; she had not taken a turn at all. "It's okay," he said. "Let's try again. I'll help you this time."

The dreamer stared into his face. She could not make sense of it all. She was in disbelief at the horror of this strange world and its strange inhabitants. Her mind was racing with confusion, and she did not want to play anymore; she refused to try again. "What's the difference? What's the benefit of one outcome over the other? I won't do it. I won't do this again. I won't play this game. I won't give myself to demons who pose themselves as choices. I won't do it."

As the dreamer protested, she felt herself slipping into a trance. The announcer began to fade, along with a crowd that had gathered. The walls of the vessel started to disappear, and her trance took her into a deep sleep; she awakened into the morning, into the reality of her home, into the familiar surroundings of the place she had been searching for from the beginning of the dream.

Printed in the United States
By Bookmasters